tarot

LEANNA GRENAWAY

SEVEN DIALS

This edition first published in Great Britain in 2017 by
Seven Dials
an imprint of the Orion Publishing Group Ltd
Carmelite House, 50 Victoria Embankment,
London, EC4Y 0DZ
An Hachette UK Company

1 3 5 7 9 10 8 6 4 2

Interior design by Kathryn Sky-Peck
Tarot card images derived from the Waite Deck created by
Red Wheel/Weiser, LLC

A CIP catalogue record for this book is available
from the British Library.

Paperback ISBN: 9781409169994

eBook ISBN: 9781409170006

Printed and bound by CPI Group (UK), Ltd, Croydon, CR0 4YY

Contents

First Steps on the Path of Tarot

1

Tarot is a popular form of divination that people have been using for centuries. By following the guidelines set out in this book, you will come to understand how easy it is to master the art of reading cards. Many people complain that many Tarot books are contradictory or too difficult to follow—and with thousands of different card interpretations in circulation, it is not hard to see why some people struggle. This book brings Tarot into the 21st century, making the card meanings easy to understand and follow. For the moment, try to forget anything that you have already picked up from other manuals and focus on the meanings set out inside these pages.

Although Tarot is primarily traditional, I offer modern and up-to-date translations for all seventy-eight cards. Afterward, you can adapt other people's interpretations where appropriate. Throughout the book, I present exercises to help you learn how to interpret groupings of the cards. To be successful in completing your knowledge, try not to skip through the book, but look at it more as a teaching manual with each chapter taking you through the process of learning Tarot.

Obviously, you will need a pack of Tarot cards, preferably ones that you choose yourself. Be sure to obtain a relatively traditional deck that has full illustrations on all the cards rather than just a collection of Cups, Wands, Swords and Pentacles. This book is illustrated with the Rider Waite Tarot, a classic and universally used deck. A Tarot deck is comprised of seventy-eight cards: twenty-two Major Arcana cards and fifty-six Minor Arcana cards.

How you store the cards is important. Purchase a small wooden box and a length of silk. Each time you have finished with your cards, wrap them in the silk and pop them away safely in their box. Some readers like to familiarize themselves with their cards and frequently bring them out to shuffle them. Another tradition is to place them on the highest shelf in the house as this is supposed to produce a more powerful influence. You could go one step further and put them under your pillow at night.

Choose your deck carefully because even after many years of reading, you will always prefer to revert to using your old faithful deck.

Am I Psychic?

We have to go back to the beginning of time—to an age when humanity's main goal was to survive. The ancients relied on their instincts because without them they were vulnerable to danger. Many were so in tune with their natural instincts that they could predict things such as weather patterns and earthquakes. The Druids and Pagans worshiped the land, studied moon phases, and became familiar with the seasons. This helped them to recognize the best time for planting and harvesting crops.

Unfortunately, much of this natural intuition has been swept away by the busy high-tech side of life. We are so consumed by technology and materialism that we have lost touch with our inner selves and the world around us. To be "psychic" means to become more in touch with your innate intuitive abilities. Get back to the basics and fill some of your spare time with meditating and reading spiritually orientated literature.

When we compare ourselves to how our distant ancestors lived, we have without doubt lost our way. But we are finally starting to realize the powerful influence of our inherent abilities. We all maintain a certain degree of psychic ability, and with concentration and dedication, we can light up the spark that lies within us all.

Tarot is the key to unlocking the psyche. Like anything that you want to achieve, the more you practice Tarot, the better you become. If I were to start an apprenticeship in plastering walls, after time I would begin to master the art. It's the same with Tarot: once you begin to understand how it works, after a while the cards will enhance your psychic flow and open your mind to a higher plane.

If you have suppressed your psychic flow, you can use the Tarot to jump-start it and to guide you. Even the best clairvoyants do not wake up psychic every morning. Anything can cause our vibration to be blocked—a poor night's sleep, stress, or even too much concentration. Even if you are not a natural psychic, the Tarot will always predict a situation, so your challenge is to learn how to interpret the cards in order to give a precise account of them. The Tarot's accuracy is spectacular and many skeptics eat their words after someone has given them a reading. Because of this, more people are finally accepting the Tarot as part of every-day life and they are consulting readers on a regular basis.

How Does the Tarot Work?

Many Tarot card readers believe in guides or guardian angels. These are our spirit companions who watch over us through-out our lifetime. There are two different types of guides. Firstly, some believe that loved ones who have passed over will continue looking out for us and that they give comfort in times of stress.

Secondly, there are the guides from the hierarchy. These spirits have reincarnated through many lifetimes in order to perfect their souls, making them capable and practical in guiding us through our life. They are known as "The Divine Beings" or spirit helpers who visit our subconscious minds and bring messages via our dream sleep.

They appear as male or female, and they are expert in steering us through certain situations. Therefore, we may have more than one guide, as throughout our lives we face many different circumstances. Some people have been lucky enough to see or speak directly with their guardian angels. Mediums do this often because they can easily create the channel of communication. A medium opens her mind to receive messages from the other side, and the Tarot does the same for those who learn to read it. The reader must interpret what the cards say and then communicate the message to the client. In many cases, some readers feel an urge to say something that is not apparent in the cards. Some use the term "vision" but it is mostly a strong feeling that the reader experiences that relates to the person for whom they are reading.

When we open ourselves to being psychic, we cannot really take the credit for the information that we relay. Without our guides assisting us, we would not be able to correspond at all. By opening our vibration, we become like a telephone line. One can describe it as being similar to tuning into a radio station. If you are mediumistic, it may take a while before the voice is clear enough to hear. If you are anything like me, you won't hear the voice of your guide speaking to you at all. This is because, for some of us, they communicate only through our subconscious, making us feel confident in our predictions. Sometimes, you may just say the first thing that pops into your head; then, low and behold, astound your client with your accuracy. Guides work beautifully with the Tarot, warning or foretelling of future happenings and giving advice through the cards. When a person shuffles the Tarot, they are not aware of the fact that they are transporting their vibration onto the cards. It is important to encourage the client to shuffle the cards for a good two to three minutes, and to concentrate on their problems while doing so. This will push the unseen energies into the cards, thus making them easier to read.

Upright and Reversed Cards

The majority of Tarot readers use the cards only in the upright position but sometimes a card accidentally lands in the reversed position. When this happens, there is usually a good reason for it. I have not gone into great detail about Reversed meanings, but I have given brief reversed interpretations for all the cards.

In some cases, it is worth looking at the upright and reversed interpretation as this shows both sides of a person or a situation— and often that is what is wanted.

A Few Tips to Help You Along the Way

Throughout this book, I will refer to the person you are reading for as the *querent* or the client.

Only read for the same person once in three months. Too many readings may confuse the querent.

Never allow someone else to conduct a reading with your cards. Only you can use your deck.

Never read for anyone if you are ill or upset. The reading may be thwarted and result in inaccuracy.

Even if the querent's cards look dismal, or if the client seems depressed, try to emphasize the positive because when a person is in a healthy frame of mind, she will find it easier to undertake complicated matters.

Don't make things up. Always say what you see. If something negative arises in a spread, follow it up with something positive, and give helpful advice on how to tackle the issues.

When performing a reading, have a source of salt nearby or light a candle. If you decide to become professional and to read the Tarot for strangers, you will get a colorful mix of individuals who will

visit you. The salt and candles will help to protect you and keep your area cleansed.

If you are female and reading for clients in your home, never let a stranger into your home without someone being there. However "spiritual" you may feel about reading the Tarot, it is just common sense to take social precautions.

Most people who visit you will have problems, and some desperate people come to Tarot readers as a last resort. Many find comfort in a reading and use it as a crutch to keep going through problematic times. Always keep a list of useful phone numbers on your table—therapists, doctors, prevention hotline numbers. With the best will in the world, you will not be able to help everyone—nor should you try—and sometimes counselors who are specialized in certain fields can make all the difference to a troubled client.

It is always a good idea to get an answering machine. Clients will telephone you at all hours wanting to follow up on their reading or inform you if something predicted has occurred, and you will have no private life if you allow this to transpire. If you use a mobile phone, and if it's possible, have one phone for your clients and one for your own personal use.

A Note to the Reader

This plain and simple book is intended to help a beginner get a good start in the art of Tarot, so it is fairly basic and very straightforward. I have included some of the traditional meanings behind the Tarot, but for the most part, I have tried to show a newcomer to the Tarot how to interpret the cards in a way that is meaningful to people who are struggling with the problems of modern life.

Rather than focus on spreads, I have included a number of exercises throughout the text that will help you hone and sharpen your skills of card interpretation.

I hope my book encourages you to learn, use, and enjoy the Tarot. I've added some tips and advice, from my own experience, for those who wish to read for others, or who may even want to go on to read professionally. Most importantly, I hope you will enjoy reading for yourself and your loved ones whenever you need a little guidance.

I have used the female gender throughout this book. This is not for any political reason but merely because I am a woman, and in my practice more women than men will seek out a Tarot consultation. It also makes a nice change!

Basic Card Facts 2

Nobody knows the origin of Tarot, and there is much mystery as to where it originated. In the 18th century, Egyptology fascinated many people, so they believed that the Tarot began its life in Egypt. We know from historical records that people used the Tarot in the Renaissance period. A deck of Tarot dating back to the 1400s was found in Milan in Northern Italy. The pack was painted for the Visconti family and was later reproduced under the name of "Visconti Tarocchi" However, the surviving decks were commonly French designs, and it was then thought the Tarot had been imported to Italy from France. If you would like to know more about the history of the Tarot, I highly recommend you read *Tarot Mysteries* by historian and Tarot reader Jonathan Dee.

Tarot has changed considerably over the centuries. Many of the earlier decks were very basic, and now they are far more detailed, with pictures more inspirational to the reader. Cards were adapted to avoid associations with the Catholic religion, changing "The Pope" to The Hierophant or The High Priest and "The Papess" to The High Priestess. In addition, the order in which the cards are placed has been modified throughout time. For instance, "The Fool," which is traditionally the first card numbered 0, originally sat at the end of The Major Arcana, making it card number 22. This occurred with many of the adaptations of Tarot. There are thousands of different decks in circulation, so some interpretations will have been adjusted differently from others.

Tarot is more popular now than ever, and it is used on a far wider scale, thus making it interesting to people from all walks of life. Initially, many used the Tarot as a card game, but it has also held a mystical and supernatural interest for centuries. It was once felt that only a few privileged individuals possessed the gift to read Tarot, but this is untrue. We all possess the ability to tune into our psyche and we are all capable in foretelling the future. While some people are born with psychic ability, others can learn to develop it. Every one of us is born with a sixth sense, and we all possess the power to tap in to our subconscious and to coordinate it.

Structure of the Tarot

There are seventy-eight cards in a deck of Tarot.

- Twenty-two are Major Arcana cards and fifty-six are Minor Arcana cards.

- All twos in Tarot represent choices and decisions.

- Apart from the five of Wands, fives tend to be bad news.

- All eights symbolize good luck.

- All Pages represent children from birth to fifteen, and these can be either male or female.

- Knights represent young men aged from between fifteen to twenty-nine.

- All Queens represent females aged over fifteen.

- All Kings represent males aged over thirty.

- The word "Reversed" means the card is upside down.

Equivalents

Suit	Other Names	Playing Card	Element	Season	Keywords
Cups	Cauldrons	Hearts	water	Spring	Emotions, relationships, friends, and marriages
Wands	Batons, Staffs, and Rods	Clubs	fire	Summer	Work, ambitions, business, and property
Swords	Daggers	Spades	air	Autumn	Health, medical, emotions, and relationship difficulties
Pentacles	Coins or Discs	Diamonds	earth	Winter	Money, cash flow, business, property, and tuition

The Court Cards

The Court cards are the Kings, Queens, Knights, and Pages and they are the trickiest cards to understand. Each has its own personality, hair, and eye coloring, and each has its hang ups. Some students find the Court cards very hard to assess in a spread, because these cards do not always represent people. They can also signify situations.

Age Ranges

Kings are men aged over thirty years of age

Queens are women over fifteen years of age

Knights are young men between fifteen and twenty-nine

Pages are male or female children aged from birth to fifteen

Coloring

The ideas here are traditional, so you can make use of them if you wish or you can go by the character of the Court card rather than any specific hair, eye or skin color.

Cups: blue to hazel eyes, light to brown hair

Wands: blue-green eyes, fair skin, fair-red hair

Swords: dark eyes, dark hair, olive/black skin

Pentacles: any color eyes, brown/black hair

If I do two spreads for the querent and the focus of the reading is her husband, he may appear as one King in one spread and another in the next. The first Court card might symbolize the person while the second indicates the outcome of the situation, perhaps the way that the husband is changing or the way that the partnership is evolving.

Significators

Before you start a reading, you can select a Court card that you feel resembles your client. This becomes the significator. You can read cards without selecting a significator, but then you have to work out whether a card that appears in the spread relates to your client or not. For example, say you are reading for a blue-eyed woman of thirty-three years and the Queen of Swords appeared in the spread, this would alert you to the fact that this is not the querent, because this Queen is traditionally dark haired and dark eyed. In this situation, you must tune into the Tarot and look at the surrounding cards to establish a story. If there is no apparent link between the Court card and the querent, it is probable that the card refers to a forthcoming situation.

For each of the Court cards, I have provided a card meaning when the card represents a *personality*, and a card meaning when the Court card represents a *situation*.

A Clever Tip

Where the Court cards are concerned, it is worth looking at both the upright and reversed meanings, as even the nicest person can have an occasional off day and behave badly, while even a nasty person can be lovely when in the right frame of mind.

Birth Signs and Timings

Twelve of the Major Arcana cards have a birth sign attached to them. It is important that you learn these, as it is the only way you will be able to add timings to your readings. The predictions that you make will usually take around six to twelve months to come about, so using the birth signs helps you to pinpoint a time.

Major Arcana Card and Birth Sign Correspondences

The Emperor	Aries	March / April
The High Priest / Hierophant	Taurus	April / May
The Lovers	Gemini	May / June
The Chariot	Cancer	June / July
Strength	Leo	July / August
The Hermit	Virgo	August / September
Justice	Libra	September / October
Death	Scorpio	October / November
Temperance	Sagittarius	November / December
The Devil	Capricorn	December / January
The Star	Aquarius	January / February
The Moon	Pisces	February / March

The
Major Arcana

3

The Major Arcana cards are the first twenty-two cards in a conventional deck of the Tarot. Many people believe them to be much older than the Minor Arcana, but there is little evidence for this—although individual images may have been around before in some other form, after which they became incorporated into the Tarot.

The images on the cards are extremely powerful and many of them offer spiritual insight to a reading. It is important to learn the meaning of these cards thoroughly, as only then can you tap into the mystery of the cards to conduct an accurate reading.

THE FOOL

Card number 0 or 22

Traditional Meaning

The young person represented in this card is sometimes known as the Jester. Fate and destiny rule the situation, as the youth is generally unaware of life's dangers.

Modern Meaning

This is quite a positive card. The card is numbered "0," which indicates a moment in time before something is about to happen. If you like, a waiting time before embarking on a new adventure. This is a starting point in the querent's life. A new path awaits her, but she must be patient as there are likely to be delays. Tell the querent she must prepare herself to take a different direction in life but not to jump in with both feet. She should stop and listen to her instincts before rushing ahead. For a time, the querent will feel insecure, and, because of this, she will find herself being thoughtless or insensitive. To see what the new path is, look at the surrounding cards in the spread. It may be a new job or relationship that is coming in or even recovery after ill health.

Reversed

Constantly feeling stuck in a rut and never moving on. The querent will go through a spell of being selfish and unpopular.

Key Points

A new path waits for the querent

An insecure time

Look before you leap

Being thoughtless or insensitive

THE MAGICIAN

Card number 1

THE MAGICIAN.

Traditional Meaning

Throughout time, The Magician has also been referred to as "The Juggler" or "The Showman." His name in the beginning was "Magus," meaning magician. He has spiritual protection.

Modern Meaning

This card carries divine occult protection. Always tell the querent that she is protected by a higher being. The querent must take a bold step forward in life using and trusting her instincts. Everything is possible when God's love is present. This is also a psychic card, so advise her to start the process of developing her psychic abilities. This can be done through meditation. Willpower and determination are needed to get through life's hard lessons, but if the querent has faith in God, the Divine Being will place his hand in hers. Even if the querent does not feel as if she is going down the right path, reassure her that she is.

Reversed

The querent may send out negative thoughts, and she must be careful that she does not attract bad luck.

She will not apply herself in the correct way, and she must change her attitude in order to succeed.

Deceit and lies will be present in her life, so advise her to create harmony wherever she can.

Key Points

The querent must use willpower to create harmony

Take a bold step forward

Use and develop psychic abilities

THE HIGH PRIESTESS

Card number 2

Traditional Meaning

This card symbolizes a female guide. Also known as The Papess. This is an exceptionally spiritual card; also considered the female version of The Magician.

Modern Meaning

She is the lady guide: the Mother or Grandmother figure in spirit. If the querent has no such relative in spirit, then a high female guide will watch and protect her. The High Priestess can appear in a person's reading if things are a little uncertain. She brings balance, promising that the fate of the querent is in the hands of the spirit world. The card itself is lucky. Good things will appear in time, so the querent should be patient and refuse to listen to naysayers. Encourage the querent to trust her feelings in all matters.

Reversed

If this card sits next to health cards, a family member might become ill. The querent should not trust others blindly. The querent may lack stamina, which could affect a relationship. Support will be needed.

Key Points

The Mother or Grandmother in spirit

Divine spiritual protection

Things take off soon

Be patient

THE EMPRESS

Card number 3

Traditional Meaning

This is the fertility card, which shows growth in all things. The growth might apply to business, love, marriage, children, and much else.

Modern Meanings

If this card appears in a reading, it usually represents the maternal figure in the family.

If you are reading for a woman of childbearing age, it could indicate a future pregnancy. Regarding pregnancy, if the querent is past childbearing age then there may be news of a pregnancy within the family. With a young female, this could warn of a pregnancy, which she may or may not want. If The Empress appears in a man's cards—a partner, daughter, or some other family member will be embarking on motherhood.

You need to look at surrounding cards to establish who might be getting pregnant. It may have nothing to do with pregnancy, but it may simply show that the querent is a solid maternal figure who takes her responsibilities toward her family very seriously.

If there are three or more Sword cards present in the same spread as The Empress, the querent or someone around her might find it difficult to conceive.

Reversed

The querent or someone close to her may have conception problems. This card in the reversed position can indicate complacency and taking things for granted.

Key Points

A pregnancy to come for the family

A maternal figure

Fulfillment and fruitfulness in some area of life

THE EMPEROR

Card number 4

Traditional Meaning

The Emperor is the father figure, and Tarot readers see him as being in control. Sometimes stern and very materialistic, he holds a position of authority, demanding respect from those around him. The Emperor is not easy to influence, and he will always follow his own judgment. He is quite Victorian and proper in his approach, and he speaks his mind. Being so matter-of-fact and occasionally judgmental can sometimes make him unpopular. In his eyes you can see that his duty is to protect all that is his.

Modern Meaning

The Emperor as an authority figure can also represent a business man. This is considered a business card, so if you have several Wands in the spread, it would be fair to suggest that the reading is work-related. Legal dealings may arise for the querent, particularly if the Justice card is also present.

Reversed

The querent will feel the weight of family responsibility. She will start projects, and then find that she is unable to finish them. She might have a thief involved in her life.

Key Points

Use Aries for timing

A boss, father figure, or authority figure

Legal or business dealings

THE HIEROPHANT

Card number 5

Traditional Meaning

The Hierophant is perceived as God's right hand man, sometimes known as The High Priest or The Pope, thus making this card extremely spiritual.

Modern Meaning

This is one of the most spiritual cards of all of the seventy-eight. This high male guide looks down over the querent throughout the journey of life. He protects marriage and family matters and steps in to ease burdens. Delays are highly featured in the querent's life, so encourage her to be patient and tell her that her guide will work for her benefit. Also, tell her to focus on spiritual matters rather than material ones, as this will help her spirit to evolve faster. The keys on the card indicate a house move and this prediction very often works. Use Taurus for timing events.

Reversed

The querent must not be afraid to undertake a new project. She should explore every avenue with an open mind.

Key Points

A high male guide in the spirit world

Focus on the spiritual rather than the material

A house move

Taurus for timing

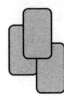

Exercise One

Memorize the twelve birth signs attached to the major Arcana. It is extremely important that you do not skip over this part, as the birth signs will become your way of predicting the time of the year in which a situation is to arise.

Study the meanings to the first five cards so that you can iden-tify them without referring to your notes. Ask a friend to test your knowledge. Memorize these cards, keep shuffling them and focus on what you can see in their illustrations.

THE LOVERS

Card number 6

Traditional Meaning

This card corresponds to the traditional Romeo and
Juliet story.

Modern Meaning

The divinatory meaning of The Lovers varies depending on the
circumstances, but, in some ways, the title to this card says it all.
The Lovers means love affairs, relationships, and sexual attraction.

If The Lovers is present in the same spread as any of the marriage cards, the couple will have a loving, stimulating relationship.
If you establish that the querent is married or with a partner,
and the Lovers falls in the same spread with any of the following cards—The Devil, The Two of Swords, The Three of Swords,
or The Five of Pentacles—the opportunity for an affair will arise.

When you are dealing with relationships of this kind in Tarot,
never confidently predict that the client will have an affair. It
comes down to her free will in the end. She may have a Brad Pitt
look-alike chasing her, but the test comes when she has to face
facts and ask herself if her present relationship is worth losing.
Even if you have recognized that the querent is terribly unhappy
in her relationship, do not assume that she will run into the
arms of a wonderful lover. Many women stay with their partners
regardless of how they are treated.

If you come to read the cards professionally in the future, you will discover that this situation is very common. Most married people will have temptation thrown in their path at some point in their life. Some will eat the forbidden fruit; others will not. Fate often tests the strongest of relationships. You may come across a married woman who is idyllically happy, but it does not mean that temptation will not test her. If the querent is already involved in a love triangle, look at the surrounding cards to see the outcome. You may see divorce, remarriage, or any number of other scenarios. If she is single, she will embark on a relationship within the next twelve months.

Reversed

There will be fighting and arguing in a relationship

Key Points

The possibility of a love affair
If the client is single, a new relationship is impending
Gemini for timing

Tip

Let us say that you see the husband behaving badly to the querent; in a situation like this you have to tread very carefully. You may be wrong, so it is best to warn the client that she might hear news of someone around her having an affair. Even if she suspects that her partner is cheating, never stick your neck out and say that he is. He may not be. If you tape your readings, he could listen to it and come hammering on your door. Be sure to safeguard yourself in every instance.

THE CHARIOT

Card number 7

THE CHARIOT.

Traditional Meaning

The Chariot is said to be the son of the Empress and The Emperor. His strength comes from his father and the spiritual blessings from his mother. His task is to steer the Chariot on its path through life, being cautious while controlling the horses in addition to controlling himself. The Chariot can decide whether he wants to be good or bad. The decision is his.

Modern Meaning

This card means travel, so imagine the Chariot upon his carriage as a form of transport. Although it is often interpreted as a journey, it is unlikely to be overseas, more of a trip by automobile in the querent's own country. Being anything from a two-week vacation to a business meeting, the travel will only last a few days. This is also the card of movement, which denotes that the querent will be able to put her plans into action and can expect things to happen suddenly. Advise her that she is in control of her time and that she must not let her life descend into chaos.

If any relationship or family cards are in the spread, quarrels and arguments lie ahead. If the querent is a man, he should control his sexual urges.

Reversed

Nothing will happen for a while

Plans and changes are on hold

Delays in travel

Problems with an automobile will cost money she can ill afford

Key Points

Travel in one's own country

Choices between good and bad

Quarrels and rows between family members

Movement and change

Cancer for timing

STRENGTH

Card number 8

Traditional Meaning

This was once seen as being a merciless card, but over time, its meaning has been toned down. This card represents man's dominion over the animal kingdom, and it reminds us that we should love and treat all animals with the respect that they deserve.

Modern Meaning

This card shows that the querent must use her strength, and may refer to physical strength if she is recovering from an illness or emotional strength if she is experiencing problems. Encourage her to give to others and to show her inner qualities of love, patience, and gentleness. Although things could be tough for a while, tell her never to give up. If she uses her strength in a positive way, all things will work out well in the end. The obstacles she encounters may not be as bad as they first seem, so tell the querent to look for solutions, face issues, and not walk away. If Strength is next to family cards then your client may be thinking of acquiring a pet.

Reversed

Someone is being cruel to animals or people. The querent gives in to basic harsh instincts. Abuse is apparent in a relationship or unfaithfulness in a marriage.

Key Points

Use strength in all areas of life

Look for solutions to problems

Never give up

Use Leo for timing

THE HERMIT

Card number 9

Traditional Meaning

This is the guiding card of wisdom and truth. The Hermit will help the querent to develop spiritually.

Modern Meaning

This card represents high spiritual protection. Someone in the spirit world is looking out for the querent. This could be a guardian angel or a father figure. Usually this card appears when the querent is going through a particularly rough time. In rare circumstances, if many negative or disruptive cards are in the spread, she may be feeling suicidal—or someone close to her could be. The querent will go through a forlorn or depressed stage, searching for companionship or for a purpose in life. Tell her to take some quiet time out to reflect on her life.

Reversed

The querent will refuse to see what is available to her. She is burying her head in the sand. She has little faith and is spiritually isolated or unaware of the spiritual side of life. She might be the type who always puts herself before others.

Key Points

Father or grandfather figure in spirit

Feeling down or searching for a purpose in life

Take some time out

Use Virgo for timing

THE WHEEL OF FORTUNE

WHEEL of FORTUNE.

Card number 10

Traditional Meaning

This card indicates the wheel of the year and the circle of life. The end is the beginning, and life is everlasting.

Modern Meaning

Many readers see this as a bad card, perceiving that life's lessons may be hard. When one problem is solved another surfaces, but life is very much like that anyway. Because of life's cruel blows, the querent might feel sorry for herself, so persuade her to understand that the world is like a big school. The lessons that she goes through are part of the spiritual plan that speeds her evolution to a higher plane of spirituality.

If you have a wealthy querent or someone who has plenty of money, she must not focus so much on the materialistic side of life. Tell her that God can take away as quickly as he gives— therefore, she must not take her monetary fortune for granted.

Have you ever heard the expression "What goes around comes around?" The law of Karma is all-important, so always be grateful for what you have.

This card can suggest that things are going around in circles for a while.

Reversed

Advise the querent not to take chances with her health if the querent is rundown or depressed.

Key Points

What goes around comes around

Going round in circles and not getting anywhere

The querent must face life's hard lessons

JUSTICE

Card number 11

Traditional Meaning

Justice can be a double-edged sword.

Modern Meaning

This is the legal card. Normally if this comes into a reading, it implies legal dealings of some kind.

Therefore, this can indicate the need to consult a lawyer, to give evidence in court, move, make an insurance claim, or cope with something similar. It can even revolve around something commonplace but irritating, such as a parking or speeding fine. Look at the cards close by to conclude the outcome of the situation.

Justice can also imply karmic payback time, so the querent's life should be kept balanced and in order. She must be honest in all she does. If she is trying to fool those around her, eventually they will suspect that something is wrong. People might try to influence the querent, so she must stick to her guns. The scales are a good representation of the sign of Libra.

Reversed

The querent will be around police involvement, crime, or criminal activities.

Key Points

A legal card

Things must stay in the balance

The querent should not try to fool others

Libra for timing

Exercise Two

Now you have some knowledge of the cards. Before you can perform a proper reading, you must learn to group the cards together. This is a bit like learning to read all over again. Some of you will pick this up straight away; while others may require a few attempts to conquer it. Don't lose heart—remember that practice makes perfect.

When you group the cards together, try to read the cards as a whole rather than singularly. If you have two cards in front of you, try to find the significator card. By this, I mean the card that seems to encapsulate a client's story or one that catches your attention. When you have established your significator card, draw in the meaning of the second one. Look at the example below:

Strength + The Empress

The Empress is the significator card as it represents a pregnancy, while Strength lies next to it. Your answer would be:

The querent will need strength in order to complete a pregnancy. A pregnancy occurs around the time of Leo—July to August.

There are many different ways to group cards together and there are various potential answers to each card group exercise. It doesn't matter if you don't reach all the interpretations at this point, just practice with a few. Here is another example:

The High Priestess + Justice

Spiritual protection surrounds the querent throughout a legal matter. Spirit will give special protection around the time of Libra.

Try this simple set of groupings and see how you go. Once you have completed them, compare your answers with those at the back of this book.

Card Groupings:

The High Priestess + The Empress

The Hierophant + The Fool

Strength + The Lovers

THE HANGED MAN.

THE HANGED MAN

Card number 12

Traditional Meaning

This card shows a man hanging by his foot from a branch with his hands behind his back. His legs are crossed in acknowledgement to God. The two trees epitomize choices. Money falls from the man's pockets implying that he is in danger of losing what he needs to survive.

Modern Meaning

Looking closely at this card, it shows that the querent has very little control over her life. She is waiting or hanging around and anticipating the future. It is important that the querent takes a step back from reality and tries to meditate to change her point of view. This is also the card of change, but although things may be slow or in limbo now, within a twelve-month period, things will change. An easier way to remember this meaning is that the querent could be hanging around for up to a year, waiting for the changes to come about.

Reversed

Trust in God and absorb earthly feelings. Be cautious with do-gooders or someone who makes empty promises.

Key Points

Hanging around waiting for change
Big things to happen within one year
Meditation is needed

DEATH

Card number 13

Traditional Meaning

Death as we know it does not exist: life is a continuing cycle of existence—birth-death-birth-death. Through life's lessons, reincarnation teaches us to evolve on to a higher level.

Modern Meaning

Before we start, this card does not symbolize death as a reality in the context of someone dying. The Death card represents the end of one chapter in life and the beginning of another. This is also the card of change—off with the old and on with the new. Nowadays when this card appears in a spread, it actually registers positive news in most readings. Traditionally, death only predicts an actual death around the querent when it is with the Nine or Ten of Swords. Let's face it; few of us go through a year without hearing that someone whom we know has passed over.

This is a card of rebirth and fresh beginnings. It can point toward the birth of a child if it is close by pregnancy cards such as The Empress. It could suggest the offer of a new job if it is sitting next to The Ace of Wands.

Many people shy away from The Death card, thinking it will predict the end of someone's life. Look at it as the end of an era and inform the querent not to be anxious if it appears in a reading.

Use Scorpio for timing.

Reversed

Total panic and disruption will be around the querent's life.

Inform her that there is a light at the end of the tunnel and that she should keep battling on.

Key Points

Changes

The beginning of a new era

A birth

Death for someone around the querent (if with The Nine or
Ten of Swords)

Dealing with Death in a Reading

Many clients panic about this card appearing in their reading and in most decks, even the look of the card can be quite ghastly and unpleasant. It is very important when you are conducting a reading to approach the subject of death sensitively. You may not know the person you are reading for, so you will not be able to judge her reaction.

When reading Tarot, I always try to encourage the "say what you see" approach, but inexperienced or insensitive readers can instill fear into their clients by predicting a death. It is actually quite rare to see death in the cards, even though we will all have to experience grief in our lives at some point. However, in the developed world in the present era, death is not as commonplace, so do not be too confident in predicting it. When approaching this subject, follow the guidelines listed below to make the querent feel more at ease.

Look at nearby cards. There may not be any grief or misery in the spread, thus suggesting that changes are more likely than losing someone. If you feel a death is imminent, tell the client that they will hear news of a death rather than indicating that they will experience one at first hand. Suggest instead that the querent may have to put a comforting arm around the shoulder of a friend. Suggest that the querent will have an opportunity to pay respects to someone who has passed away but without shedding any tears. This way, the death does not play on the client's mind. Should the querent go on to lose someone dear to her, she will appreciate your honesty in bringing the matter out in the reading—even though you did not "have it quite right."

Never say the words, "I can see a death in the cards" because you might implant the idea that someone the querent loves will die. Believe me, some people's imaginations can run wild! Never assume there will be a death or feel confident enough to predict this. You are not God, and you may be wrong. If you are uncertain, say nothing at all, or say that this card means that a particular situation is ending and that it will make way for a new one. In a way, then, the Death card says what it means—that is, that something will die away in order for something new to come in.

If you go on to be a professional reader, you will find that most of the people who come to see you will be in the middle of some dilemma. Their lives are likely to be upside down or particularly difficult at that time. Although it is important to read the cards in a divinatory fashion, it is also equally important not to send the querent away feeling worse than when they arrived. If you do this then you have failed as a reader.

Death is a funny issue. Everyone deals with it differently. Some clients may be nervous or uneasy, and this can distort the reading in their mind. Always downplay the idea of actual death and send the querent away with hope in her heart.

TEMPERANCE

Card number 14

Traditional Meaning

This represents spiritual knowledge along with cleansing and harmony.

Modern Meaning

This could represent a guardian angel. Reassure the querent that spirit is protecting her and looking after her at all times. Destiny has a hand in everything she does, so even if things are not as clear as she would like them to be, in time the answer will come. Temperance also represents patience, self-control, and discipline. It may indicate unbalanced mood, so the querent should weigh people and situations carefully. Use Sagittarius for timing.

Reversed

Emotional frustration will cause stress. This is not the right time to begin new projects. The querent shouldn't waste her time by trying to do the impossible. A conflict in business leaves the querent searching for changes.

Key Points

The guardian angel is watching
Comparing two situations
Patience

THE DEVIL

Card number 15

Traditional Meaning

The devil thrives on man's imperfections and feeds off negative energies.

Modern Meaning

THE DEVIL .

This is quite a complicated card and not a particularly nice one. In some decks, this card is called Temptation, hence the idea of weakness or lust. Greed or perversion is not always the case, but the card can point toward the fact that the querent will be in contact with someone who is cunning.

Relationships or marriages could face problems and in some cases, they might end. If this card lies close to a number of Swords, there may be violence in a partnership or at the very least, verbal abuse. If The Lovers card is in close proximity, sexual perversion or an element of kinkiness could be evident in a relationship, although I doubt that any reader would ever have the guts to come out and say it! If this card is close to a relationship card, it is doubtful that the affair is a healthy one.

There can be health issues here in connection with the head, or the possibility of mental illness. I have also heard it said that this card indicates skin diseases or something that causes itching—connected with the idea of burning in hell!

Reversed

An exceptionally bad character lurks around the individual. Danger is near so tell the querent to ask for spiritual protection.

Key Points

Greed, perversion, and lust

Being around someone who isn't very nice

Poor health relating to the head, mental illness, or the skin

Capricorn for timing

THE TOWER

Card number 16

Traditional Meaning

Lightning is striking and people are falling from grace.

Modern Meaning

As you can see, this is quite a disruptive card. Things in the querent's life could become difficult, and there will be many obstacles ahead. This can relate to break-ups in relationships and friendships, alongside arguments, fights, and quarrels. To forgive is hard, but try to encourage the querent to see things from a different perspective. Changes will come along and these will bring about a new awareness. Sometimes the querent may be in for a spate of ill health or she may hear of an accident.

Reversed

Head injuries or accidents. Depression and disaster.

Key Points

Break-ups in relationships and friendships
Accidents and poor health
Quarrels and arguments

THE STAR

Card number 17

Traditional Meaning

This denotes the giving and receiving of gifts, also a person who doesn't seek material wealth.

Modern Meaning

This is the highest, most spiritual card of all. The Star represents guidance from above—the kind that is more powerful than any other kind. If The Tower is next to The Star, a female spiritual guide will watch over and protect the querent from anything bad, but she must meditate and try to understand a spiritual faith in more depth. This is also the humanitarian card, meaning that the querent will help others by giving them hope and inspiration. Wishes and dreams will be fulfilled in time.

Reversed

The person will show a lack of faith, but she has no need to worry.

Key Points

Highest card of protection
This is humanitarian card, so the querent should help others
Aquarius for timing

Exercise Three

Try the following card groupings; the answers are in the back of this book:

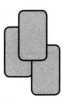

The Emperor + The Star

The Devil + The Lovers

Death + Temperance

THE MOON.

THE MOON

Card number 18

Traditional Meaning

This card, by tradition, shows both good and bad, but both are in the shadow of moonlight.

Modern Meaning

Things are not as they seem. In some decks, this is called the card of illusion. Look deeper for undercurrents and deceit. The querent must listen and trust her instincts, for she will be right in the end. Situations around the querent may not be open and obvious, or someone close could be concealing a secret. Advise her not to be too trusting and to look closely at what others are doing so that they do not take her in by lying to her. The individual needs to be cautious of idle gossip, and she must not believe everything she hears.

If the querent is female, and if there are health cards in the spread, she may encounter some gynecological problems. For a male, there may be stomach ulcers. Use Pisces for timing.

Reversed

A mystery will be solved after a long wait. Beware of secret enemies.

Key Points

Lies and deceit

Secrets surround the client

Female—gynecological problems

Male—Stomach ulcers

Use Pisces for timing

THE SUN

Card number 19

Traditional Meaning

The powerful rays shine down on all.

Modern Meaning

This is unquestionably the best card in Tarot, followed closely by The Ace of Cups, as a predictor of good things. Whatever is happening in the querent's life, and no matter what obstacles she faces, the outcome will be a happy one.

If the Sun is in the same spread as a relationship card, romance will thrive. If it is around cards of health, then a full recovery can be expected. If The Sun is near cards that indicate poverty or money problems, extra cash will come in. This truly wonderful card promises that all things will work out well in the end.

Tip

It is rare to see The Ace of Cups in the same spread as The Sun, but should you see this, everything will be magnificent, and the querent should expect amazingly good fortune.

Reversed

There could be a risk of fire, but this will not result in anything too serious.

Key Points

Totally positive in every way

Things improving

The best card in the deck

With The Ace of Cups something glorious will occur

THE WORLD.

THE WORLD

Card number 21

Traditional Meaning

Victory, strength, intelligence and the Seeing Eye, along with spiritual power.

Modern Meaning

This card symbolizes perfection and completion. This is a highly successful card, as it brings victory and all good things with it. This also suggests travel, which is easy to remember as it indicates travel around the world. Usually the travel is associated with foreign trips or vacations, but not always. I sometimes use this card to tell the querent that the world is her oyster and that she should not be afraid of taking a chance. Victory and success is noticeable in her future.

Reversed

The querent is in a rut and she cannot see what lessons she must learn. Advise her to change her life.

Key Points

Success and victory
Travel, usually abroad
Perfection
The world is your oyster

Exercise Four

This exercise is a little more difficult because you will have more cards to deal with, but don't let that put you off. Just like before, find the significator and group the cards together. You will find the answers in the back of the book.

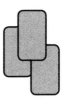

The Fool + Lovers + The Sun

Death + The Magician + Strength + The World

The Emperor + The Empress + The Charioteer + The Tower

The Suit of Cups

4

This is the first suit of the Minor Arcana. These cards give the details that bring a reading to life. They fill in the gaps and allow you to stretch your imagination, making each reading individual. There are fifty-six cards in the Minor Arcana and these are the four suits of Cups, Wands, Swords, and Pentacles.

The suit of Cups is the nicest of all the four suits. It focuses mainly on relationships and family matters, giving meanings to all types of situations. A number of Cups gives a positive slant to a spread of cards, and it often brings lighter aspects to a sad or harsh reading.

ACE OF CUPS

Card number 23

Traditional Meaning

A gift from the heavens, stillness and serenity.

Modern Meaning

This is the second-best card in the Minor Arcana. Very soon, the querent will experience joy and peace. You will need to look at the surrounding cards to ascertain the reason for her good fortune. If bad cards are at hand, then this card will bring about a happy outcome to a current problem. The querent will hear of a pregnancy or she will celebrate someone's engagement or wedding. All will be well because this is a truly wonderful card.

Reversed

Things have not always been the way they should be, but with hard work, good fortune will come along.

Key Points

The second-best card in the deck
Births, weddings, engagements, and celebrations
A happy outcome

TWO OF CUPS

Card number 24

Traditional Meaning

Some traditions suggest pregnancy.

Modern Meaning

Some say that this is the card of soul mates or two extremely compatible individuals. If the querent is single, then a wonderful new romance is on the way. She will be comfortable in her relationship and compatible with her partner. The unity will be sexy but also based on truth and honesty. The couple communicates very well, making it not just a physical connection but also a blending of the minds. This card points toward an impending marriage or engagement and a pregnancy.

If you are reading for a person who has split up from her partner, there should soon be reconciliation.

Reversed

A breakdown in relationships.

Key Points

Wonderful connection between mind and body

Reconciliation

Engagement, marriage, or pregnancy

THREE OF CUPS

Card number 25

Traditional Meaning

Eating, drinking, and having a good time.

Modern Meaning

This is a joyous card. Parties and celebrations will be evident in the coming year for the individual with births, weddings, or other occasions coming along. It is also the card of a family reunion. Any problems in the querent's life will soon conclude, so tell her not to worry. If your querent is romantically unattached, a new love affair will lift her spirits. If the querent is married or in a relationship, everything will be rosy.

Reversed

Love for the wrong reasons, too much sex, and not enough communication. If the querent overindulges with food and drink, her weight will rocket. Difficult people are around the querent, and there is backbiting within the family.

Key Points

Celebrations in the family or with friends
Problems solved
New love affairs or harmony in marriage

FOUR OF CUPS

Card number 26

Traditional Meaning

A "couldn't care less" attitude.

Modern Meaning

The querent or someone close to her is dissatisfied and thinking that the grass must be greener on the other side. A family upset is expected, maybe in a relationship, or there may be problems generally in the family. Help and encouragement will be offered from an unexpected source, giving her a much happier outcome than she expects.

Reversed

The querent will feel like giving up, and she could let a great opportunity pass by her. Tell her to try to make new friends and get out more.

Key Points

Family upsets or problems with relationships
The querent must try to be grateful for what she has
Help and support is at hand

FIVE OF CUPS

Card number 27

Traditional Meaning

Feelings of regret and unhappiness, but a chance
to rebuild.

Modern Meaning

Most Cup cards are happy ones, but this one is
depressive, especially if it is with relationship cards. A separation
is likely for the querent; children may be involved. She will regret
her past actions and want to turn the clock back. This also means
unrequited love.

If this card sits next to work or financial cards, a business will
crumble or money problems will cause despair. Sometimes, and
only rarely, the client or someone associated to her could feel
desperate or suicidal.

Reversed

The querent will be meeting people from the past. May indicate
a move.

Key Points

Looking into the past
Regret, intense sadness
Problems with business or money
Unrequited love

SIX OF CUPS

Card number 28

Traditional Meaning

A woman declines a man's offers.

Modern Meaning

A reunion is likely. Perhaps a love affair from the past that will be rekindled, or a relationship will be reconciled. There are definitely conflicts and arguments, and the man may be trying to win over the woman. If the querent is divorced, it is possible that there will be an upset around the custody of a child or arguments over money.

Reversed

A small inheritance or windfall. A person who refuses to grow up.

Key Points

Relationships from the past
Reconciliation
Conflict and rows around relationships
Marriage disputes over custody
In young people, an innocent affair

SEVEN OF CUPS

Card number 29

Traditional Meaning

A mixture of events will occur, but the querent's soul is growing karmically.

Modern Meaning

This is a very spiritual and psychic card. Tell the querent to interpret or write down her dreams, because she will find it easy to connect with her spirit guides. She may find herself experiencing some psychic visions.

Prepare her for changes because there will be many choices for her to make in the coming year, which in turn will take her on to a new learning curve. Positive things are ahead, so looking forward to these experiences will open a new chapter in her life.

Reversed

Same as upright.

Key Points

Choices and decisions
Listen to dream sleep
Await new beginnings

EIGHT OF CUPS

Card number 30

Traditional Meaning

Running away from the past. All Eights in Tarot predict good luck.

Modern Meaning

When this card appears in a spread, your client may be looking back into the past too much and not living for today. It is also the card of moving on and taking a different direction. If The Lovers or The Two of Cups are close by, the client may have to think about whether she wants to remain in—or leave—a relationship.

A blonde woman will come into the life of the querent. Look at the additional cards in the spread to decide whether she is good or bad.

Reversed

Feeling sorry for oneself. A very selfish and egotistical person.

Key Points

Moving away from situations
New beginnings
The querent must not live in the past
All eights in Tarot bring good luck and hope

Exercise Five

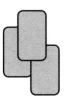

To help you group four or more cards together, look at the example below. Remember that Tarot readers can interpret the cards in many ways, so if you do not reach exactly the same answers as I have put in at the back of this book, don't worry. Your version will probably work for you because there is no real "right and wrong" in Tarot interpretation.

Interpretation One

The Hanged Man + The Tower + Ace of Cups + Seven of Cups

There will be a few problems around (The Tower) lasting for approximately twelve months (Hanged Man). Many decisions will be made in the next year (Seven of Cups), but all will be well in the end (Ace of Cups).

Interpretation Two

Periodic headaches will affect the querent for around a year (Tower + Hanged Man). These are not serious and they will disappear eventually (Ace of Cups). These headaches may occur in connection with a difficult pregnancy (Ace of Cups + Tower).

Interpretation Three

Difficult times (The Tower) will force the querent to look more deeply into her spiritual side (Seven of Cups). This brings about changes in the next twelve months (The Hanged Man), which will produce a happy outcome (Ace of Cups).

Now give your interpretation to the following cards, keeping your answers brief, informative, and to the point:

The Lovers + Wheel of Fortune + Six of Cups + Eight of Cups

Death + The Fool + Two of Cups + Seven of Cups

Five of Cups + The Moon + The Charioteer + Strength

NINE OF CUPS

Card number 31

Traditional Meaning

The Romany Gypsies call this "The Wish Card."

Modern Meaning

Being the wish card, this is truly positive. Whenever this comes out in a spread, it illustrates that the client's wishes will be granted. Give her hope in foretelling that her future will be joyful and that a celebration is at the forefront. Tell the querent to wish for what she wants, as in time she will get it. Some readers like to ask the querent to make a silent wish upon the card.

Reversed

Overeating, drinking, and weight gain. Others take advantage of the querent's hospitality or good nature.

Key Points

Make a wish

Celebrations

Abundance

TEN OF CUPS

Card number 32

Traditional Meaning

A happy family, joy, and purpose.

Modern Meaning

This card denotes a good relationship or love partnership. The couple may have had difficulties, but now they find happiness and stability. They will still have to work at their marriage though, because life often brings about difficulties. If the lovers make an effort, they will be happy, successful, and even more closely united than they are now. If you are reading for a single woman, then you can predict this relationship for her future.

The card can also predict a windfall when next to the Nine of Pentacles. This may be only a very small amount of money or goods, but it could be huge. Only predict a large win if you are certain about it.

Reversed

A family upset will result in a child running away. Romantic tiffs and squabbles will go on for at least six months. If next to The Nine or Ten of Swords there will be news of a death.

Key Points

    Relationship and marriage card

    A windfall or a large win

    Bad relationships in the past

    True happiness comes after hard work

PAGE of CUPS.

PAGE OF CUPS

Card number 33

Traditional Meaning

This card represents a child who might have blue or hazel eyes and fair or mousy hair. Naturally, the coloring would depend upon the race. In some decks, this Page represents a girl, but, traditionally, Pages can be either sex.

Modern Meaning

The child is connected to the querent in some way, so this might symbolize a child that she has now or one that she will have in the future. If this were not possible due to the age or condition of the querent, then it would represent a relative such as a niece, nephew, or grandchild.

Personality

This Page is sweet natured, and she will not usually bring any problems to the family. She will love her home life and be sociable with friends and relations. She will not be particularly academic and could struggle a bit at school, but later in life she will get by and go on to hold a practical position in employment.

The Page of Cups usually enjoys projects such as the arts or a gentle form of sport. This might include dancing, singing, music, the arts, stage, theatre, martial arts, pool, or billiards.

This is a very psychic young person, so tell the querent to

expect her to have imaginary friends or talk about God and angels from an early age. The card talks about an endearing little person that any family would be proud to include in it.

As a Situation

This card represents a course, lessons, and learning something new that might be artistic or creative.

Reversed

Signifies a change in a child's character

Key Points

- Can represent a female child in some decks
- Has a tendency to be psychic
- A child who enjoys mild sports and the arts

THE KNIGHT OF CUPS

KNIGHT of CUPS.

Card number 34

Traditional Meaning

This card represents a young man between the ages of fifteen to twenty nine. In white races, his eyes are usually blue to hazel and his hair color can be either sandy blonde or mousey.

Modern Meaning

This young man is a favorite with women due to his charm and good looks. He oozes charisma and can usually have any girl he chooses. He is rarely faithful to his partner and will have left a trail of heartbroken females in his past. Being highly sexed, racy, and smart, he's the "love them and leave them" type who is not opposed to over indulging with drink and drugs.

Personality

This young man might have a history of trouble with the law. He may also have a poor school record because he could not (or would not) concentrate on academic matters. He is a loveable rogue who in time will eventually follow the right path. His generosity ensures that he has many friends, but he will not be as faithful to them as they are to him.

In many cases, if the querent is a mature woman, this is a son.

Always give hope for the future for this Knight as he rarely turns out to be a bad person in the end.

As a Situation

This card represents visitors, company, visiting friends, day trips, and outings.

Reversed

The Knight of Cups will lose his lover to another man. If two or more male character cards are present in a spread with the Knight of Cups, he has to fight for something or he feels threatened in some way.

Key Points

A womanizer
An unfaithful lover
Dabbling in petty crime
Drugs and fast cars
A change of character in later life

QUEEN of CUPS.

THE QUEEN OF CUPS

Card number 35

Traditional Meaning

This Queen is usually blue-to-hazel eyed with light brown hair, depending upon racial considerations. Her age can range from fifteen plus.

Modern Meaning

This is a mature woman with a loving, gentle personality. She is a maternal figure, enjoying home life and children.

Personality

The Queen of Cups can sometimes be too soft, so she allows others to take her good nature for granted. In certain cases, she has been divorced and will only find her true love later in life when she has become stronger in her opinions. She shows fondness for animals and a love of nature. She has great perception with brilliant intuition, and her common sense will always lead her away from trouble. She will not welcome outsiders immediately, but once you have won her confidence, she is a friend for life.

As a Situation

This card indicates a social life that picks up and good times with friends on the way.

Reversed

This card can relate to a horrible mother-in-law or stepmother. A gossipy and interfering woman who exaggerates all the time.

Key Points

Lovely natured maternal figure

Love of animals

Love of home, creature comforts, and children

May be divorced

THE KING OF CUPS

Card number 36

Traditional Meaning

This man has blue to hazel eyes depending upon his race. He has an air of authority about him.

Modern Meaning

A strong and powerful image, the King gives accurate advice while counseling others. Sometimes inconsiderate in marriage, quiet and noncommunicative, far different from the man we see at work.

Personality

A private person who keeps his thoughts very much to himself, he gives little of his inner self away, even to his nearest and dearest. He will have to try harder with marriage and commitment, as his wife may find him dull and boring. However, he is a reliable father who is solid and steady, and in some cases, religious.

This King is ambitious, and he is accountable in business. A strong and powerful personality, he gives accurate advice and counsel to others, although he sometimes puts others down. Outside the workplace, he keeps his private thoughts and life very much to himself, and he gives little away.

As a Situation

New male friends are likely, but these acquaintances will be short-lived.

Reversed

A marriage cheat. A controlling and manipulative man. A man's man who likes to drink with his friends.

Key Points

Ambitious, responsible
Noncommunicative, dull, and boring
A father figure

Exercise Six

Incorporate the Court cards and see how you interpret them in the following card groupings:

The Queen of Cups + The Empress + The Star

Knight of Cups + Three of Cups + Justice +The Devil

Queen of Cups + Page of Cups + The Tower +The Sun
+ The Hermit

The Suit
of Wands

5

Recognized in most decks as Rods, Batons, or Wands, this suit is associated with work, career, and business matters. If more than three Wands appear in the same spread, the querent has her career, business, job, or even a voluntary occupation in the forefront of her mind at the time of the reading.

ACE OF WANDS

Card number 37

Traditional Meaning

One single Rod sits in the centre of the card. In some decks, branches grow from the Rod to symbolize growth and rebirth.

Modern Meaning

All Aces in Tarot are optimistic, and this card is always pleasant to see in a spread. This gives the querent a new beginning or discovery to look forward to, as it always signifies something good. In most cases, this can be a new job or a new start in property or business. If the Ace is among other Rod cards, it could relate to a situation around work (look to surrounding cards to establish whether they are good or bad). This card can also predict fertility or a possible birth.

Reversed

A block or delay.

Key Points

A brand new job or business venture
Fertility and birth

TWO OF WANDS

Card number 38

Traditional Meaning

The wisdom to make the correct choices in life.

Modern Meaning

As Twos in Tarot represent choices and decisions, this card can indicate the need to make a serious decision at work or business. A new venture is ahead, but it is up to the querent to take up the challenge or leave it alone, as it does not appear to be a matter of destiny. Sometimes this can suggest the querent will need to make a great effort at work, especially if disruptive cards are present in the spread. The querent may contemplate buying something new like a new vehicle or an expensive gift for someone else.

Reversed

Have patience because delays and setbacks are imminent. The querent will lose interest in work or business and mundane tasks will become boring.

Key Points

Choices in work and business
Struggles and problems
Purchasing new things or buying gifts

THREE OF WANDS

Card number 39

Traditional Meaning

This lifts the spirits.

Modern Meaning

The querent may help or support a friend or relative. The energy that she expends by propping up those around her will make her feel worn out and tired. Carrying people through difficult times is fine up to a point but not if it is sapping the querent's own energy. If you are reading for someone who cannot stand up for herself, she will seek help and support from others, but she will rarely act on the advice that they give her.

Another meaning to this card is that work and business will improve. In some cases, work brings travel.

Reversed

The querent is wasting her talents and listening to bad advice.

Key Points

Advice and support given or received

Improvements in career, work, and business

FOUR OF WANDS

Card number 40

Traditional Meaning

A home or the security within it. There is usually some indication of family life with this card.

Modern Meaning

In some Tarot decks, this card is associated with marriage or a relationship where the people are living together. As Wands represent work, this relationship may need hard work for it to succeed. There may have been difficulties in the past or they may occur in the future. The couple can repair past damage if they are prepared to make an effort. Encourage the querent to fulfill her ambitions and to count her blessings.

Reversed

Relationships will fail. The querent is spending too much money.

Key Points

Marriage or committed relationship
Hard work improves a relationship
Fulfill ambitions

FIVE OF WANDS

Card number 41

Traditional Meaning

A diversity of opinions.

Modern Meaning

There are problems and battles at work. Colleagues around the querent are outraged about work mat-

ters, and there is no peace, quiet, or harmony. This represents a trying time. Encourage the client to be strong and not to submit to bullying or backstabbing. Life may be unpleasant for a while.

Reversed

The querent is at her very lowest, but things will improve. She must leave things as they are or walk away from them. She can try and sort things out in her present situation or find a new one later.

Key Points

Battles at work
Bullying and backstabbing
Colleagues up in arms

SIX OF WANDS

Card number 42

Traditional Meaning

Victory and acclaim.

Modern Meaning

The querent may have had tough times in the past and she may still be struggling. The surrounding cards will show what the problems are, but whatever they might be, this card predicts victory to follow. Ensure the client that her difficulties will be short-lived.

This can also mean good news coming—or buying or exchanging an automobile. If the card is among many Sword cards, it can mean problems with a vehicle.

Reversed

Victory is delayed or lost. The querent may want something that belongs to someone else.

Key Points

Struggles at first, victory to follow

Good news to come

Changing vehicles, or automobile problems

SEVEN OF WANDS

Card number 43

Traditional Meaning

Thought and consideration.

Modern Meaning

This card can refer to two opposing ideas, one being
redundancy and the other being a promotion. If bad
cards surround this card, the meaning is loss and redundancy, but
if positive cards are present, the card predicts a promotion. If the
querent cannot foresee a promotion happening in her current
occupation, this indicates a change of job that takes her higher up
the ladder or one that pays better. Encourage her not to walk away
from her difficulties but to face them because only then will all be
well.

This card can also indicate that the client will soon be teaching or training others—that is, transferring information to others.

Reversed

An embarrassing incident. Someone may try to show the querent
up or make her feel small in front of others.

Key Points

Promotion or redundancy
Teaching or training
Learning to face difficulties

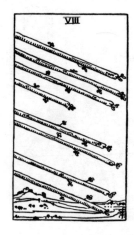

EIGHT OF WANDS

Card number 44

Traditional Meaning

Nature and time.

Modern Meaning

This is one of the travel cards but mainly it refers to air travel. Even though Wands usually represent work, this journey is likely to be for pleasure, so the querent may soon be able to take a well-deserved vacation. A house move also works with this card, so you could predict that the querent will not always stay where she is now.

When you apply this card to a work situation, it means advancement unless the card is reversed. Changes are coming, but they will move slowly at the start and speed up later.

Reversed

Strike action at work. The querent cancels a vacation. Jealousy at work. Arguments.

Key Points

Journey by plane

Changes coming swiftly after a long wait

A house move

Advancement or problems at work

Exercise Seven

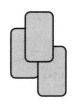

Ace of Wands + Two of Cups + Three of Wands

The Tower + Five of Wands + The Star

The Moon + Four of Cups + Six of Wands

Read the first three cards as though you were doing a three-card grouping exercise. Then read the second three cards, then the third three cards. The last card suggests the outcome. Another easy way to read a spread of this kind is to group the suits together. If one row contains all three cards from one suit, read the story that the group shows you. Another idea is to find a significator card and build the reading around that.

NINE OF WANDS

Card number 45

Traditional Meaning

Protection in case the querent needs to defend herself.

Modern Meaning

This is the card of caution, so the querent must be on her guard. A time-waster or sneaky person will be among the querent's or her partner's friends. Look at the other cards in the spread to determine the situation and the outcome. Small groups of people could gang together to bring the querent down.

Reversed

A person in the family might have a drinking or drug problem.

Key Points

The querent must be on her guard

Time-wasters are around

Groups ganging up against the querent

TEN OF WANDS

Card number 46

Traditional Meaning

Determination to see a project through to completion no matter what.

Modern Meaning

The querent needs to keep her nose to the grindstone for awhile because she will need to work hard in order to finish a task or to please her superiors. At work, someone may ask her to take on extra responsibility, and she could find others taking her for granted. If this Wand appears around relationship cards, her partner steps up the pressure and leaves her feeling emotionally and physically exhausted. This can sometimes mean that the client is in a dead-end job.

Reversed

Waiting for a promotion. A stolen legacy. Broken bones or injuries.

Key Points

Hard work and toil

Taking a lot of responsibility

Pressure, not getting anywhere at work

THE PAGE OF WANDS

PAGE of WANDS.

Card number 47

Traditional Meaning

A Page who has help from the gods.

Modern Meaning

In most decks, this Page can be either male or female, but very often The Page of Wands is a young boy from the age of birth to fifteen.

Personality

A lovely inquisitive child, easy to manage, and with a lively nature. This could be the querent's son or a relative. Listen to what this child has to say because he could be the bearer of good news.

As a Situation

News, correspondence, or writing something important.

Reversed

Illness, bad news, and rumors fall heavily on the querent's shoulders. Childish pranks and impatient friends.

Key Points

> Fair haired or light eyed
> Enjoyable child related to querent
> Good news is ahead

THE KNIGHT OF WANDS

Card number 48

Traditional Meaning

Aggression and battles.

Modern Meaning

This Knight has the gift of gab and is a somewhat
cocky character, but he is also rather traditional. The Knights
of Wands and Cups can sometimes be erratic, but they tend to
settle down in later life.

Personality

During his late teens and early twenties, he will change jobs frequently, hop in and out of bed with a variety of partners, and he
will carry on regardless without a care in the world. Sometimes
his rather senseless attitude lands him in hot water.

His excellent conversational skills ensure that his opinions
are sometimes fixed or inflexible, so others see his lack of tact as
offensive. The truth of the matter is that he is a nice young man
who will blossom when he reaches full maturity.

As a Situation

Travel and communication, especially for business purposes.

Reversed

An insecure young man who breaks promises. This represents a person who cannot resist temptation.

Key Points

Blonde to brown hair where appropriate

Light eyes where appropriate

Restless with frequent job changes

Traditional views

Chatty, gift of the gab

Could occasionally put his foot in his mouth

THE QUEEN OF WANDS

Card number 49

Traditional Meaning

A light-eyed woman.

Modern Meaning

The Queen of Wands is generally nice with a love of nature and animals—she will probably have a houseful of pets.

Personality

She loves her home and makes a near-perfect wife and mother. Green issues interest her, and she is always prepared to do her share for any good causes that arise. If her partner does not give her the attention she needs, she could be prone to flirt or even to embark on an affair, but her partner will have to push her to the extreme for her to go this far.

As a Situation

The querent will take advice and then make sensible business or financial decisions.

Reversed

A fast and loose woman who is temperamental and fickle. No interest in family life.

Key Points

Sincere, lovely woman

Blue-eyed where appropriate

Red/blonde hair where appropriate

Loves animals and nature

Good wife and mother

Could be prone to an affair in extreme cases

THE KING OF WANDS

Card number 50

Traditional Meaning

A spiritually developed man.

Modern Meaning

This King is pleasant and generally liked by all. He is an honest, reliable, amusing man with a witty personality.

Personality

He is sweet natured and especially geared to his family and friends, and is usually faithful; but like the Queen, will always need to be kept interested romantically. This King is intelligent and does well at work or in business. He is an excellent boss or employer and is fair and sympathetic. At best he shares the decision making with his partner, but he can be weak willed at times and happy to leave her to make all the decisions. He is a great father, and his wife can rely on him, but he can be a bit soft and allow their children to run riot. A daughter could wrap him around her little finger.

As a Situation

There will be communications and negotiations that lead to success.

THE FOOL.

Reversed

This man could be a liar with a devious and unreliable attitude. Lots of broken promises and arguments within the family.

Key Points

Fair to brown hair

Blue or grey eyes

Intelligent, reliable, amusing, and witty

Good father and husband but a little soft at times

Usually faithful

Exercise Eight

Try the following groupings, but this time see how many different interpretations you can come up with for each set of cards:

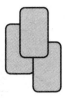

King of Wands + Two of Wands + The Lovers + The Devil

Queen of Wands + The World + Ten of Wands + Justice

The Sun + Ace of Wands + Seven of Wands + Queen of Cups

The Suit
of Swords

6

Unfortunately, this suit is rather depressing because Swords represent conflict, illness, and tension. If someone is going through a particularly bad time, many swords can be present in a spread. It is always best to follow a "difficult" reading with something positive; otherwise the querent will go away with little hope.

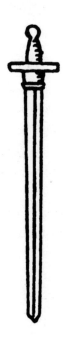

ACE OF SWORDS

Card number 51

Traditional Meaning

Justice on higher levels and great spiritual action.

Modern Meaning

This card tells us that the querent has recently endured trouble or hardship and may be down in the dumps—or in extreme cases—depressed. She has learned some valuable lessons through these difficult times and now victory will follow. Give your client hope if you feel that she is dejected, and tell her that she will soon discover that her life is back on track. This card links with hospitals and operations, especially when the Five of Pentacles is in the spread. If the Tower appears too, this Ace may signify a wound that needs stitches.

Reversed

Fate and destiny will take their course. Making wrong decisions. Delays and shocks.

Key Points

Struggle at first but victory follows

If next to Five of Pentacles, this means an operation

If next to The Tower, stitches to a wound

TWO OF SWORDS

Card number 52

Traditional Meaning

Tradition calls this "the divorce card"!

Modern Meaning

At some point in the future, the querent will experience severe relationship problems. A once-happy marriage or partnership starts to turn sour, and a hopeless outcome for the relationship is inevitable. An infidelity or future infidelity will take place if The Lovers, the Three of Swords or The Devil is in the spread. The querent must sit down and make a conscious decision as to whether she will continue with the relationship. Whatever she decides, the outcome will definitely end in a break in the relationship.

It is worth noting that this scenario can also apply to a business partnership or even to a project that the querent should off-load.

Tip

If you hope to be a professional reader, be very careful when making predictions with this card. You could be reading for someone that has just embarked on a new romance or recently entered into marriage. In many cases, this card carries a long-term prediction. The querent may still be in love, so telling her that the relationship will eventually end could upset her unnecessarily. A good way to use this card is to say that her relationship will include some difficulties and that later on she will have to make decisions as to how it is to continue. Even though you may know that the end is near, it must always be the querent's decision to break up. Never predict that her partner will leave her.

Reversed

Do not be pushed into making a decision.

Key Points

Divorce or separations in relationships

Choices and decisions

Blocked situations

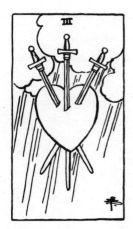

THREE OF SWORDS

Card number 53

Traditional Meaning

Tradition tells us that this is "the adultery card."

Modern Meaning

This is only the adultery card when the Lovers card appears in the same spread. The querent does not have to be married, because she may just live with someone. If you are going to predict adultery, always state that it is the querent's decision to remain true or to be false. Although the spirits may bring someone new into her life, this is a test for her, and it is her choice at the end of the day. She does not have to embark on an affair because she has the option to walk away from it. This sad card indicates that the querent is not happy and that her life could continue to be miserable for a while.

If this Three of Swords is next to the Empress, there may be news of a miscarriage. If it appears with cards that talk about health matters, someone around the querent may have heart problems or angina.

Oddly enough, an alternative meaning can sometimes indicate a house move.

Reversed

Loneliness and confusion.

Key Points

Adultery, if with The Lovers

With cards of health—heart problems

Empress—miscarriage

Upset and misery

A house move

FOUR OF SWORDS

Card number 54

Traditional Meaning

Separating oneself from the world outside.

Modern Meaning

This is one of the many health cards as it supposes that the querent or someone close to her is convalescing. It does not necessarily talk of a serious illness, as this is more likely to be a virus or minor problem. However, she will still retreat from the outside world, probably by taking time off from work. This is also a waiting time, so it is essential that the querent is patient. Fate will control everything in the end, so assure the querent that the future is in the hands of the spirit world.

Reversed

Put life on pause for a while and learn to be patient.

Key Points

Convalescing at home

Taking time off due to minor illness

Fate and destiny rules and controls, so learn to be patient

FIVE OF SWORDS

Card number 55

Traditional Meaning

The querent must change things for the better—not all is lost.

Modern Meaning

This card relates to health. It may indicate a time of mental strain or pressure that leaves the querent living on her nerves for a while. This card may also indicate anger and hostility. Often the root of this problem is a relationship, so the querent may suffer mental or physical abuse from a partner. People may spread gossip about the querent, or there may be family arguments. In rare situations, it can indicate a burglary or break-in. A positive aspect of this card says that an admirer will show up within a twelve-month period.

Reversed

Doom and gloom. Ignoring good advice.

Key Points

Mental or nervous health problems
Family arguments, gossiping
Violence or abusive arguments around relationships
Burglaries
An admirer

SIX OF SWORDS

Card number 56

Traditional Meaning

Things will be brighter ahead.

Modern Meaning

This card is associated with movement, which could imply moving, changing a job, changing a relationship, or just moving on to better things. You can predict that the querent will move out of her current area—perhaps only a few miles away or to a distant place. The Six of Swords can represent an overseas vacation, especially if other travel cards are around. This card signifies the end of problems with soothing times ahead.

Reversed

Delays around a house move. Delays around travel or postponing vacations.

Key Points

A move out of the area

A holiday and better times ahead

SEVEN OF SWORDS

Card number 57

Traditional Meaning

Tradition considers this a card of criminality or of cloak and dagger events.

Modern Meaning

This is not a nice card as it can mean theft, which can be anything from a burglary to a snatched purse, a swindle, or some other kind of loss. If this card is around Pages, it points toward a child who is stealing. Once again, be cautious when predicting a burglary. Some people may panic at the thought of this, but the client may simply hear of a break-in rather than have one herself.

This card also denotes jealousy. Someone around the querent may be envious or vindictive, but he will be clever enough to hide his true colors. Warn the client about false friends or manipulative colleagues.

Reversed

Things which were lost may turn up. Making up with a loved one.

Key Points

Theft and deception
Trickery and jealousy

EIGHT OF SWORDS

Card number 58

Traditional Meaning

Not being able to see the truth.

Modern Meaning

The querent will be in a very confused state of mind, knowing inwardly that something is wrong but not wanting to confront the situation. This usually indicates relationship difficulties or work problems. Karmically speaking, these tough lessons will make the querent face up to her weaknesses and become stronger as a result. There may also be a female around the client who wants to hurt her or to exact revenge.

Reversed

The querent should keep her chin up and all will soon be well. Negative feelings fade.

Key Points

Feelings of being trapped
Confusion
A female is out for revenge
Karma, learning spiritual lessons

Exercise Nine

Now try to make a reading out of the following groups of cards:

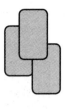

Four of Cups + Six of Swords +Two of Swords + Justice

Ace of Cups + Four of Swords + Eight of Wands + The Star

The Chariot + Five of Swords + Two of Cups + King of Wands

NINE OF SWORDS

Card number 59

Traditional Meaning

Things that we cannot control.

Modern Meaning

This card can mean death, but the same rules apply here as they do for the Death card in the Major Arcana. Actual death is only relevant when the card falls next to The Tower, which means a sudden death—perhaps from a heart attack or a car crash. This situation is very rare so you are unlikely to see this combination often. Because the reading is so extreme, you must play it down where possible. When the Nine of Swords appears without The Tower in the same reading, the querent will feel trapped or circumstances around her will appear to be hopeless. She could also experience problems in connection with a mother or mother-in-law.

Reversed

A rainbow after the storm. Good news coming at last.

Key Points

Death if the Tower is also present

Hopeless situations

Problems with mother or mother-in-law figure

TEN OF SWORDS

Card number 60

Traditional Meaning

Tradition calls the Ten of Swords a "death card."

Modern Meaning

I regard this card as the worst one in the deck because it gives very little hope. If this appears in a reading, you should concentrate on the surrounding cards. If The Ten of Swords and The Death Card appear anywhere in the same spread, then the death of someone or something is highly probable. On its own, it can mean financial loss resulting from either bad luck, redundancy, or, in exceptional situations, even bankruptcy. Ill health could be a factor. Try your best to give hope to the querent and always follow through with something positive.

Reversed

A karmic debt has been paid. Hope and encouragement. Spiritual protection throughout bad times.

Key Points

Ten of Swords with The Death card implies a death

Ill health, hospital, and sickness

Financial loss

Misery

THE PAGE OF SWORDS

Card number 61

Traditional Meaning

A child is ready for battle.

Modern Meaning

This Page can be male or female. This individual tends to be willful and full of his own opinions. He can also be stubborn, and he may find discipline hard to accept. His parents will constantly battle to gain control of him, and at times, they will be at the end of their rope. In some cases, the child may have a hyperactive disorder like ADHD. This child might have a spiteful nature, which will get him into hot water with teachers and those who have to take care of him. In teenage years, he might get into trouble with the law!

Personality

It really does depend on how you wish to interpret this child's card when doing a reading. You may feel that he is just somewhat excitable—for example a very young child who is going through the "terrible twos." However, he will always be a handful, and the querent will need to guide him along the correct path in life. His good qualities are that he gives a lot of love and that he will grow up to be a very capable person.

As a Situation

Important news is coming, or the querent will sign a contract or other important document.

Reversed

Try to understand a sick or mentally ill child who might be handicapped or mentally challenged.

Key Points

Child's nature—difficult, hyperactive, naughty, and opinionated
Can be either male or female

THE KNIGHT OF SWORDS

KNIGHT of SWORDS .

Card number 62

Traditional Meaning

Strength of mind.

Modern Meaning

A fearless, confident man with little or no conscience.

Personality

When he sets his mind to what he wants, he will stop at nothing to achieve his goals and does not care whose toes he must step on. He is deep and mysterious and does not allow anyone to get close to him. He is sexual and extremely passionate. As with most of the Knights, this young man tends to be rather full of himself.

As a Situation

Travel, possibly without much prior warning, also last minute arrangements and quick decisions.

Reversed

Wait and be patient.

Key Points

Dark in coloring

Mysterious, deep

Sexual, passionate, and ambitious

Journeys and travel

QUEEN ♣ SWORDS.

THE QUEEN OF SWORDS

Card number 63

Traditional Meaning

A dark haired woman who has an edge to her nature.

Modern Meaning

Although this woman can have a sharp tongue at times, she is the type that seems to have everything under control.

Personality

She is a strong, self-sufficient woman who is in tune with most things around her. She is career orientated and enjoys her work. She is nobody's fool and tends not to trust men much. Men admire her because she has physical beauty as well as spiritual beauty. She may have had previous difficulties in her life and has become cynical. She does have a gentle side and tends to be a well-balanced mother, giving her children the independence they need and the chance of finding their own way in life.

As a Situation

There may be conflict, and the querent may have to stand up for herself against difficult people.

Reversed

Intolerant, interfering, oblivious to others' opinions.

Key Points

Strong, career orientated

Has had a hard life

Doesn't trust men

A well-balanced mother

Divorced or widowed

KING of SWORDS.

THE KING OF SWORDS

Card number 64

Traditional Meaning

This represents true justice.

Modern Meaning

This man is usually a popular, well-liked individual who is intellectual and generally at the top of his profession. Because of his capabilities in dealing with company politics and his extreme determination in all he does, the King of Swords will always thrive in business. This card can also correspond to professionals, such as doctors, teachers, or members of the armed forces. He is not particularly spiritual but shows no skepticism either.

Personality

This man is usually a popular, well-liked individual who is intellectual and will always be at the top of his profession, as he is capable of dealing with company politics and he is determined in all he does.

As a Situation

The querent will consult a lawyer, doctor, builder, or someone who has special knowledge or skills.

Reversed

A bully who misuses his power. A stern husband or father. Disloyal and secretive.

Key Points

An admired man

Dark eyes, dark hair

Political rather than spiritual

Exercise Ten

Lay one card down as a significator and then a row of three beneath it. Follow with two more rows of three and one final row containing one card. Write down your interpretations. Avoid being long-winded, just use this test in a basic manner in order to get you off the ground.

The Suit
of Pentacles

7

In many decks, the designer calls this suit Coins or Discs. This suit is associated with money, study, and work. The Pentacles rarely predict severe or long-term problems. If you see more than three Pentacle cards in a spread, the querent might have a thirst for money or she might simply be in business or dealing with financial and business matters.

ACE OF PENTACLES

Card number 65

Traditional Meaning

Wealth in return for past efforts.

Modern Meaning

This is the best money card in Tarot. Even if unpleasant financial cards are in a spread, this card

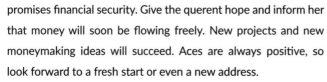

promises financial security. Give the querent hope and inform her that money will soon be flowing freely. New projects and new moneymaking ideas will succeed. Aces are always positive, so look forward to a fresh start or even a new address.

If this card appears with the Wheel of Fortune, then the querent will receive a legacy or some money through an insurance claim. Next to the Nine of Pentacles, a large lump sum of cash will turn up. In rare cases, this can denote a lottery win, but this combination can equally apply when a person sells a house.

Reversed

Greed, materialism, and poverty.

Key Points

> Financial gain, success
> A new project
> Lump sums if with appropriate cards

TWO OF PENTACLES

Card number 66

Traditional Meaning

A young man tries to balance two Pentacles in an attempt to balance his financial affairs.

Modern Meaning

This is not a good card for money matters, because it means that the querent must pay attention to her bank account. Money will be short for a while, and she will find herself juggling cash. Fortunately, the period of hardship is likely to be short lived, so when this card shows up, be sure you give your client plenty of hope for the future. Twos in the Tarot represent choices, and in this case, the querent will need to make decisions about money—changing credit cards around for a better interest rate or renegotiating mortgages and loans. This card also indicates various kinds of communication.

Reversed

Legal problems and hold ups. Broken promises. Financial changes for the better.

Key Points

Juggling money through tough times

Robbing Peter to pay Paul

Letters and communications

THREE OF PENTACLES

Card number 67

Traditional Meaning

A young person works hard in order to make progress.

Modern Meaning

This card often signifies self-employment. Not everyone for whom you read will be freelance or have their own business and not all will wish to do so. However, when this card appears, the querent is likely to be self-employed and supporting herself financially. If your client is self-employed or wishes to become so, look at surrounding cards to decide upon the outcome. This is also the "apprenticeship card" so your querent may be learning new tasks or attending college or university.

Reversed

Family rows over money.

Key Points

Self-employment
Financial self-support
College, university, or apprenticeships

FOUR OF PENTACLES

Card number 68

Traditional Meaning

This shows the need to keep the majority of one's money safe and spend only a little.

Modern Meaning

The querent must not overspend. Uncertain times may be on the way, so advise her to keep her cash safe. Alternatively, the querent could be around a person who has a preoccupation with money or someone who is stingy or miserly. If this is next to a travel card, it could indicate failing a driving test.

Reversed

Loss of money. Hard work for little reward.

Key Points

Do not overspend

Someone being mean or greedy with money

A failed driving test with travel cards

FIVE OF PENTACLES

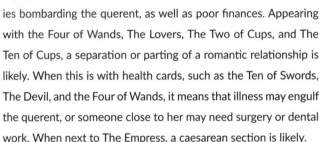

Card number 69

Traditional Meaning

Feeling as though one is out in the cold.

Modern Meaning

This is a complicated card. When the Five of Pentacles is alone, it suggests worries and anxiet-

ies bombarding the querent, as well as poor finances. Appearing with the Four of Wands, The Lovers, The Two of Cups, and The Ten of Cups, a separation or parting of a romantic relationship is likely. When this is with health cards, such as the Ten of Swords, The Devil, and the Four of Wands, it means that illness may engulf the querent, or someone close to her may need surgery or dental work. When next to The Empress, a caesarean section is likely.

If more than one of the above cards appears with this Five, it is best to use only one interpretation.

Reversed

God is making the querent face a karmic lesson.

Key Points

Financial poverty

Operations and surgery

Separation within a relationship

SIX OF PENTACLES

Card number 70

Traditional Meaning

Weighing up a financial situation.

Modern Meaning

This card is reasonably good. Although there will not be any shortage of cash in the client's future, she must still take care not to overspend. The querent tends to be slightly over generous, perhaps spending too much on others. On a negative note, warn the querent against lending money or goods, as anything that she lends will be a long time coming back, if it ever does!

Reversed

Legal problems might occur. Someone may be trying to buy a friendship. An indication of throwing good money after bad. Unpaid debts hang around.

Key Points

> Spend some, save some
> No major problems with money
> Never lend money because it may not come back
> The querent is being too generous

SEVEN OF PENTACLES

Card number 71

Traditional Meaning

Looking toward the future and hoping for the best.

Modern Meaning

The client might be worrying needlessly over money. Assure her that spirit will protect her.

However, advise her not to take on any financial commitments within twelve months, as she could struggle to pay back loans. If this card is next to a Page, the querent might be around a very naughty child.

Reversed

Waiting for change to occur. Broken promises over money.

Key Points

Needless concern over cash

Money gained through hard work

Warn against taking out loans

Around Pages, this could relate to naughty children

EIGHT OF PENTACLES

Card number 72

Traditional Meaning

Accomplishments but also continued efforts.

Modern Meaning

This is the card of study or course work, and it shows an individual learning a new task. If you have established that the querent has children, her youngster may be taking exams or attending college or university. Look closely at the surrounding cards to determine success or failure. On the other hand, this could mean that the querent will take up further education, or she may take courses relating to work.

Reversed

The querent could have trouble with her ego. Failure of exams and courses.

Key Points

Course work, study, and exams

New learning experiences

NINE OF PENTACLES

Card number 73

Traditional Meaning

Wealth.

Modern Meaning

This is a fabulous money card. Cash will come in, either in the form of a lump sum or in an ongoing

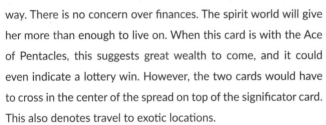

way. There is no concern over finances. The spirit world will give her more than enough to live on. When this card is with the Ace of Pentacles, this suggests great wealth to come, and it could even indicate a lottery win. However, the two cards would have to cross in the center of the spread on top of the significator card. This also denotes travel to exotic locations.

Reversed

The querent could be the victim of her own wealth. Money is good but there is no love in the querent's life.

Key Points

Brilliant finances
Money coming in abundance
Lump sums and lottery wins

TEN OF PENTACLES

Card number 74

Traditional Meaning

Financial security.

Modern Meaning

This relationship card concerns people who live together as a couple. Usually the pair will have struggled emotionally or financially in the past. However, their relationship is so strong that it can withstand the knocks in life. They will eventually enjoy financial reward and have little or no worry over money. Such a relationship is so strong that even if the spread contains the Two of Swords, they will hear of someone else's divorce rather than having to face one of their own. If the Ten sits beside a group of Court cards, a family reunion or celebration is highly starred.

Reversed

Problems with pensions and insurances. Taxation difficulties. Legal and financial problems.

Key Points

Relationship or marriage card
Financial security
The querent is able to take life's knocks
Family reunions

THE PAGE OF PENTACLES

Card number 75

Traditional Meaning

Financial security.

Modern Meaning

This child is mostly quiet and studious, the type
who enjoys reading and learning. School will be important to him,
so he will do his best to achieve high standards and good grades.
This is the most intellectual of all the Pages, so this youngster will
have a good education and a good career to follow.

Personality

The coloring of this Page is debatable. He could be blond, brown-
haired, and light eyed or dark eyed. Tradition suggests that the
Pentacle family is blond but as Tarot has progressed, a modern
approach has replaced this strict code.

As a Situation

There may be a small bonus, a small raise in salary, or a small
windfall.

Reversed

Bored, moody children with wasted talents.

Key Points

A studious child who is interested in learning

College or university later

THE KNIGHT OF PENTACLES

Card number 76

KNIGHT of PENTACLES.

Traditional Meaning

A desire for financial gain.

Modern Meaning

This Knight is a conscientious man who has worked
and trained hard to achieve his goals.

Personality

He is a clever, academic individual but he may not have reached
his full potential, so there is still time for him to further his education. In his teens, he will show little interest in women owing to
shyness, caution, or lack of sexual nerve. He will soon catch up
though, leaving all the other Knights standing, and will go through
a phase where he will be a real Romeo with many girlfriends.
The difference between this Knight and the others is that he will
respect women and treat them well. In later years, he will be successful in business or his career and will be a high achiever.

As a Situation

Finances and business improve, but the querent will need to exercise caution. This card also represents journeys.

Reversed

This Knight may be arrogant and unrealistic, so he needs to come back down to earth.

Key Points

A clever and academic young man

At first cautious in romance, but he will catch up

He will become a high achiever in business

THE QUEEN OF PENTACLES

Card number 77

Traditional Meaning

Maturity and continuity.

Modern Meaning

This woman has social grace, intelligence, and elegance. Her interests lie in the arts, environmental issues, and charity.

Personality

She is usually an influential woman with good business sense. Her main fault is that she can be bossy, especially toward her children. Her thoughts run deep, making her hard to fathom.

As a Situation

There will be growth in business, career, finances, or the money to spend on something important.

Reversed

This woman will marry for money. An interfering woman who gossips in society.

Key Points

Love of the arts and charities

Influential and inclined to be a bit bossy

THE KING OF PENTACLES

Card number 78

Traditional Meaning

A symbol of authority.

Modern Meaning

This King is an attractive person who has established a certain position in life. He is in a position of authority and respect, and he is known for his efficiency and hard work.

Personality

He started at the bottom of his career and worked his way up, but it is also possible that he inherited his position or his wealth. He may be a financial advisor or may work with figures and finances on a daily basis. He has a down-to-earth nature and a wonderful sense of humor. His parenting skills are good, and he makes a very loving husband and father.

As a Situation

Success in business, finance or property matters.

Reversed

A corrupt and perverse man who cannot be trusted.

Key Points

A man of high standing

He is respected at work and at home

A kind, down-to-earth father

Reading
the Cards
for Others

8

There are thousands of ways to lay out the Tarot, and now that you have explored the meanings of the cards, I encourage you to explore the many Tarot books available that discuss card spreads. You will find that the Celtic Cross is among the most popular. But in this plain and simple book, my focus has been on helping you understand the cards themselves, as well as giving you exercises to boost your understanding. Here are a couple of simple card spreads that you can experiment with.

Basic 9 Card Spread

Place the cards in three rows of three and using what you've learned about reading cards in relationship to each other, start with the top row, then interpret the second row, and finally the third row. Take one more card to show the outcome.

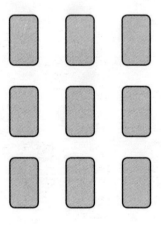

The Sun Dial

This spread is called the Sun Dial. Lay down a significator card and one more to sit across it, then take twelve cards and lay them in a circle round the two central cards like the numbers on a clock. This reading will predict what will be happening to the querent in the near future. Turn the first two over and then turn each of the other cards over one by one. This gives the querent a general twelve-month reading. Another variation of this circle layout uses two cards for each month of the year, starting with the month that you are in. This is an excellent spread for someone who wants a general twelve-month forecast.

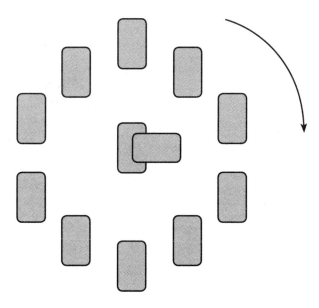

You and Your Client

Whether you are hoping only to read for your friends and family or you hope to become a professional Tarot reader, it is important to learn how to verbalize your predictions. A good approach at the beginning of a reading is to tell the querent that the Tarot cards show overall situations and that they do not always give dates and times. This means that the querent may not understand everything that is contained in the reading, but assure her that it will make sense later. Tell her to keep an open mind because some of the things that appear in the cards may take six to twelve months or even longer to come about.

Engage Your Client

Many readers stick out their necks and try too hard. For example, by saying to the querent, "I see you have a daughter" puts you in a vulnerable position. It is far better to be less definite and say something like, "The cards tell me that you may have a little girl in your life." If the querent already has a daughter, she will usually say so. After this, you can examine the surrounding cards to establish whether they relate to this child or not. Sometimes the client will say that they have a son; in this case, the card is actually picking up on the boy's sensitive and artistic nature.

The cards are rarely wrong, but if you make a mistake in your interpretation by being too confident, or stating something too categorically, the client will go away thinking that you don't know your business. If you engage the client by discussing the *possibilities* of what you see, she will usually confirm, or fill in the missing pieces. Put everything in the future tense or in the conditional tense; this is the safest approach. For instance, "I can see a change of address here, but it may not have happened yet."

Don't Fish

There is nothing worse than going to a Tarot reader only to have him or her ask endless questions. Never ask a direct question, because this is completely unprofessional.

Do not say, "Do you work?" "Are you married?" "Is your father dead?" The querent will not be impressed. This is fishing, and readers who use this approach do not get many recommendations from their clients.

For example, you can say, "You have lots of work-related cards in your spread: does this mean anything to you?" By telling the querent there are work cards, you are predicting the fact that she will be in employment. The querent may tell you that she is not working at present, in which case you would go on to tell her that the cards indicate possible work in the future.

The Sad Client

Sometimes clients visit Tarot readers because they have problems that make them unhappy. They are looking for answers. Your main goal is to guide these people and to lighten their load. Always bring about a positive outcome without making things up. In most cases, problematic situations do improve in time, and it is important that you make this clear. After hearing this, your client will often start to take a positive attitude. As a reader, you will often be asked for your opinion, but be cautious and think before you speak. A sad client is a vulnerable client; you will have a profound influence on her, so proceed responsibly with your comments.

If you feel that your client is significantly depressed and is seeking a Tarot reading out of desperation, do not read for this client. Gently refer her to an appropriate resource for help.

The Silent Client

This is quite frustrating and common. A person will arrive for a reading and they will sit stony faced throughout. Once you have established that they want you to conduct the entire reading without opening up, there is little that you can do. Put every-thing in the future tense and try not to let the client get to you. If you are really struggling, tell the querent that they have a force field around them and that they should relax so you can proceed. Another good approach is to ask the client if she feels that you have predicted something that has already happened. This usually breaks the ice. The chances are that once you make one or two "direct hits," the client will then relax.

The Motor-Mouth Client

This one is actually much worse than the silent client. A number of people sit and talk all the way through a reading. It will be difficult for you to get a word in edgewise.

You may mention something about her husband, and she will go on to tell you all about his job, his ex-wife, and his bad back. In fact, she will tell you all the things that you can clearly see in the reading. These readings can last for ages and when the job is done, you will feel drained. These people obviously love company and like to chat. It might be the only reason they have booked in to see you in the first place. You may feel like telling them to hush up, but it's best to let them rattle on.

The Obstinate Client

About one in every ten people you see will be pig-headed, rude, and disrespectful. Oftentimes these people seek out a Tarot reading on a lark, just to see what this "pyschic stuff" is all about. They may come in with an attitude and take great pleasure in watching you squirm. The typical scenario is to disagree or laugh at everything you say, or to shake their head every time you make a future prediction. Remain professional and calm and never lose your temper.

You can battle on regardless with the reading, but this can be exhausting. Alternatively, you can say that you feel they are on a negative vibration and that you cannot possibly conduct a reading for them. The obstinate client hates this, so she will usually start to behave. If you do send the client away without a reading, never charge them. In most cases, they nearly always try to book in again with you, but this time with an open mind.

Should I Charge for My Readings?

The simple answer to this is "yes." Being psychic is a gift. Over time, you will do your fair share of free readings, so charging a small fee for your time is not asking too much. Find out what the local going rate is and then offer your readings at a similar or slightly lower price. As you become more experienced, you can charge more. There is another side to charging that is very important. For some strange reason, the client takes the reader more seriously if she has to pay for it.

Answers to the Exercises

9

Exercise One

The Emperor = Aries

Hierophant = Taurus

The Lovers = Gemini

The Chariot = Cancer

Strength = Leo

The Hermit = Virgo

Justice = Libra

Death = Scorpio

Temperance = Sagittarius

The Devil = Capricorn

The Star = Aquarius

The Moon = Pisces

Exercise Two

The High Priestess + The Empress

If the querent is of childbearing age, a pregnancy is probable. If not, then she will hear news of a pregnancy. The High Priestess suggests that she will be spiritually protected throughout the course of motherhood.

The Hierophant + The fool

A new path waits for the querent, and this will be blessed. The change could involve a house move, or depending on surrounding cards, it will take place around the time of Taurus (April and May).

Strength + The Lovers

There are three potential interpretations for this exercise. If you have one answer right, you have done well.

A new relationship around July and August (the sign of Leo)

Strength will be needed in a relationship

Strength will be needed around Gemini time (May and June)

Exercise Three

The next three readings each have two potential interpretations.

The Emperor + The Star

Around January to February, the querent will be close to an Aries man, perhaps a boss or father figure.

The highest form of spiritual protection surrounds the querent around the time of Aries.

The Devil + The Lovers

The querent has the opportunity for an affair, but this relationship does not look good. Perhaps the man is aggressive or violent.

The querent will suffer health problems relating to the head at the time of Gemini (May and June).

Death + Temperance

Changes occur around the time of November and December.

The end of one phase in life and the beginning of another, so the querent must be patient.

Exercise Four

The Fool + Lovers + The Sun

A fantastic relationship is coming to the querent somewhere down the line.

Death + The Magician + Strength + The World

Major changes face the querent in the next twelve months, and these might take her traveling abroad. She will need to be strong and to trust her instincts.

The Emperor + The Empress + The Charioteer + The Tower

Tradition calls the Charioteer the son of The Emperor and Empress. This grouping could indicate that problems and arguments surround family members.

Exercise Five

The Lovers + Wheel of Fortune + Six of Cups + Eight of Cups

Reconciliation is offered to the querent from either a past love or a present one. The Wheel of Fortune suggests that things will probably not change, and it may be best for her to walk away. This could happen around Gemini time.

Death + The Fool + Two of Cups + Seven of Cups

The querent needs to make choices concerning a matter of love. She will have to make decisions as to whether she wants to move on or not.

Five of Cups + The Moon + The Chariot + Strength

Problems surround the querent, and she will need to muster some strength to overcome her difficulties. Someone is not telling the whole truth. This may be a partner or spouse. Feelings of depression and unhappiness may engulf the querent for a while, but brighter days will come and support is on its way.

Exercise Six

The Queen of Cups + The Empress + The Star

At the time of Aquarius, the querent will either become pregnant or hear of a pregnancy. The star predicts that she will be spiritually protected.

The Knight of Cups + Three of Cups + Justice + The Devil

A young man, whom the querent knows well, must be kept under observation. He may have dealings with the law or be up to no good. If she is embarking on a relationship with this man, she must take care because he will drag her down with him. His birth sign could be either Libra or Capricorn, otherwise this situation could arise at around the time of October to January. Because the Three of Cups is present, it is doubtful that anything really harmful will take place.

The Queen of Cups + Page of Cups + The Tower + The Sun + The Hermit

The Queen may have some problems with a disruptive child or be concerned about his health. There is spiritual guidance coming in from a man who is in spirit and The Sun promises a happy outcome. Suggest August to September for timing.

Exercise Seven

The Ace of Wands + Two of Cups + Three of Wands

The querent will have to make decisions about taking a new job. If she finds it hard to choose, she will benefit from taking advice from others.

The client will ask for advice from close friends or family about a new relationship.

The Tower + Five of Wands + The Star

Around January to February, arguments and upsets besiege the querent. These could be associated with family or work. Because The Star is present, her spirit guides are keeping an eye on the situation.

The querent could be battling with colleagues at work or staff might be in up in arms about certain issues. As a result, she may suffer from stress-related headaches.

The Moon + Four of Cups + Six of Wands

Around the onset of spring, lies and deceit causes an upset in a relationship. The Six of Wands shows a happy end to the situation.

There will be problems involving a vehicle. The Moon suggests that the querent think carefully before purchasing any new form of transport as she could end up with something faulty or impractical.

Exercise Eight

The King of Wands + Two of Wands + The Lovers + The Devil

The King could embark on an affair that is problematic or abusive. Struggles are ahead and he will need to make decisions.

The King will have a bout of ill health that could cause him problems around the time of May and June.

Queen of Wands + The World + Ten of Swords + Justice

A vacation could go badly for the Queen, perhaps resulting in sickness. She may pursue this legally when she returns.

A legal situation will cause the querent grief, but after a time of anxiety, success will follow.

The Sun + Ace Wands + Seven Wands + Justice

A promotion is highly starred for the querent or for someone close to her, resulting in a change for the better. Suggest September to October for timing.

The querent will pursue a legal matter, and this will result in a new beginning and a happy outcome.

Exercise Nine

Four of Cups + Six of Swords + Two of Swords + Justice

The querent is feeling despondent, as she appears to be in a relationship that has become quarrelsome. She may think the grass is greener on the other side and want to escape the situation at home. If she does not handle this delicately, the marriage or relationship will fail, leaving her seeking legal advice. Timing is likely to be September to October.

A divorce causes the querent to move away from the area.

Ace of Cups + Four of Swords + Eight of Wands + The Star

Around the time of January to February, the querent will suffer a minor health problem. Because the Ace of Cups is present, all will be well. Good times are on the way, and a lovely vacation will be welcome.

Celebrations are in the air and these might include an engagement. After a quiet period, the querent will move home, perhaps with her new partner. The Star promises that spirit will bestow blessings on her.

The Chariot + Five of Swords + Two of Cups + King of Wands

A good relationship with a kind and reliable man might turn sour after a barrage of arguments and upsets. The querent may have to take some action, because the Two of Cups represents her relationship, but the reality is that this is probably only a minor blip.

Reconciliation occurs between two soul mates after a disruptive time in their relationship.

Exercise Ten

This is a sample reading for a twenty-two year old woman

The Knight of Swords + The Tower + The Lovers +
The Knight of Wands + The Three of Swords + The Five of
Wands + Ace of Wands + The High Priestess +
The Queen of Cups + The Star.

First, take The Queen of Cups as your significator.

There are two Knights in the spread with the Three of Swords and The Lovers, so you can assume that she will have the opportunity for an affair.

The Tower and the Five of Wands would indicate that relations with one Knight could be problematic and that she is unhappy.

The High Priestess and The Star are present, so she will receive help from spirit when she makes decisions.

The querent is feeling desperate in her romantic situation because arguments and quarrels dominate her life. In time, another young man (Knight of Wands) will enter her life, and she will have to choose whether to stay with her present relationship or move on to another. It is likely that she will be attracted to the second man, as The Lovers and the Three of Swords together suggest that it will be more than a passing fancy. New beginnings are there for the taking, and if the querent has any difficulty in deciding what to do, she must ask her guide for help. The situation could occur around January to February or at the beginning of the year.

Try another practical guide in the
ORION PLAIN AND SIMPLE series

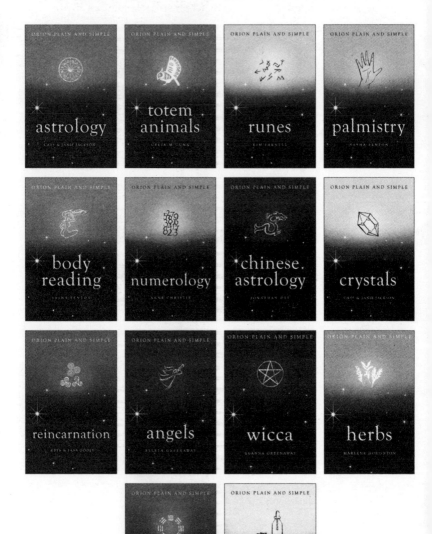